Content

Introduction 6

Chapter 1. Vision, Mission & Strategy 8

    Satya Nadella putting his mark on Microsoft 9

    Microsoft´s Paradigm Shift 11

    Windows becoming the Edge of the Cloud: 12

    The Four Platforms 13

    Beyond the Cloud 14

    Conclusions 15

    Lessons for Partners 15

Chapter 2. Microsoft´s Business Model Changes 17

    The Satya Era: All about Cloud & Services 18

    Conclusions 20

    Lessons for Partners 21

Chapter 3. Co-opetition 25

    How competing has changed under Nadella 25

    Competing in the cloud world 26

    Competing in the AI world 28

    Conclusions. 29

    Lessons for Partners 29

Chapter 4. The Microsoft Culture 32

    The Nadella Effect 32

    Conclusions 34

    Lessons for Partners 35

Chapter 5. How Microsoft organizes 37

    The Microsoft organizational setup and the cloud world. 39

    The Commercial Sales Organization 39

    The One Commercial Partner Organization 42

    Conclusions 43

    Lessons for partners 44

Chapter 6. The Microsoft Partner Strategy 46

    Introduction 46

    A unique partner sales model 47

    Different partner types 47

    Pre-Cloud partner Business models 48

    Microsoft´s partner strategy summarized 51

    What should a partner do? 51

    Conclusions 52

    Lessons for partners 53

Chapter 7. Required knowledge to partner with Microsoft. 55

    The Microsoft Partner Network 55

    Microsoft Competencies 56

    Licensing 57

    The Cloud Solution Provider Program 59

    Channel incentives 61

    Conclusions 62

    Lessons for partners 62

Chapter 8. Working with Microsoft Consulting Services . 65

    Conclusions 66

Lessons for Partners 66

Chapter 9. Define your strategy 68

    ISVs 68

    The Modern Partner 71

    The Distributor 78

    The Asset Heavy provider 78

    Conclusions 79

    Lessons for partners 79

Chapter 10. Operationalize 82

    Operationalizing your strategy with Microsoft 82

    Plan, Execute & Govern 88

    Conclusions 91

    Lessons for partners 91

Chapter 11. Best Practices & Challenges in working with Microsoft 93

    General best practices 93

    Conclusions 97

    Lessons for partners 97

Acronyms 100

Introduction

This guide is most abbreviated version of my book 'Refresh the Road Ahead' which I published in July 2018.[1]

In that book I go deep into things like the Microsoft strategy, organization, culture, etc. and, I reflect in detail on the outcomes and learnings of interviews with 40 award winning Microsoft partners.

Refresh the Road Ahead is a book of over 450 pages in its paperback version and close to 100.000 words, which for some people is a stopper to dive into the book. With this version I have tried to make a summary guide that can be read in 60 minutes.

This guide is intended for companies and individuals that want to start partnering with Microsoft. It will help you understand how to build or transform your business together with Microsoft.

If you are an existing Microsoft partner you will probably not find any new learnings in this guide.

---

[1] It is about 15% of the total word count of Refresh the Road Ahead and therefore very simplified compared to Refresh the Road Ahead.

I hope you enjoy the guide and feel free to connect on LinkedIn https://www.linkedin.com/in/-mvv-/ or on Twitter @michielvvliet.

Happy Reading!

Michiel van Vliet

Madrid, August 2018.

Chapter 1. Vision, Mission & Strategy

Depending on your age, you might still remember one of Microsoft's first mission statements, **a PC on every desk and in every home**.[2] This was all about democratizing computing for the masses, from consumers to Small and Medium Business to large corporations.[3]

During the Ballmer era, the Microsoft mission was **to enable people and businesses throughout the world to realize their full potential.**

With the reorganization that Ballmer started in July 2013, Microsoft moved to **creating a family of devices and services for individuals and businesses that empower people around the globe at home, at work and on the go, for the activities they value most.**

How did the Microsoft mission change under Nadella? Microsoft moved from being a devices and services company under Ballmer to being **the productivity and platform company for the mobile first and cloud first world** under Nadella.[4]

A common mistake that people made at the time was calling Microsoft's mission Mobile first, Cloud first. Satya

---

[2] Nadella in Hit Refresh, his book that came out in Oct 2017, refers to this mission statement more as a goal than a mission statement "A computer on every desk and in every home, which Bill and Paul had introduced forty years earlier as the company's mission, was actually more of a goal—an inspiring one for its era"
[3] You will see Satya Nadella use the word democratizing quite a lot. The latest incarnation is in democratizing AI for the masses.
[4] In Hit Refresh chapter 3, New Mission, New Momentum Nadella explains the journey of how he came to establish this mission.

has always stated that Mobile first, Cloud first is a **World View**. The mission was being the productivity and Platform Company.[5]

Satya Nadella putting his mark on Microsoft

Fiscal year 2015 was Satya´s first full fiscal year at the helm. Some refinements in strategy were the regrouping of the reporting structure around **three interconnected ambitions; Reinvent productivity and business processes, Build the intelligent cloud platform** and **Create more personal computing.**[6]

---

[5] Nadella in Hit Refresh, chapter 3: "Worldview is an interesting term, rooted in cognitive philosophy. Simply put, it is how a person comprehensively sees the world—across political, social, and economic borders. What are the common experiences we all share? The question I had been asking before becoming CEO, why do we exist, forced me to change my tech worldview, and, similarly, now every leader at Microsoft was changing theirs as well. We no longer lived in a PC-centric world. Computing was becoming more ubiquitous. Intelligence was becoming more ambient, meaning computers could observe, collect data, and turn that feedback into insights. We were seeing an ever-increasing wave of digitization of our life, business, and our world more broadly. This was made possible by an ever-growing network of connected devices, incredible computing capacity from the cloud, insights from big data, and intelligence from machine learning. I simplified all of this and encouraged Microsoft to become "mobile-first and cloud-first." Not PC-first or even Phone-first."

[6] Microsoft's fiscal year starts in July.

Organizing the financial reporting around the Three Ambitions. July 2015 – June 2016

On September 29, 2015, Microsoft announced changes to the way it reported its financial results in order to be more aligned with the three interconnected ambitions. The new reporting structure aligned with how Satya organized the business and how Microsoft thinks more about **ecosystem monetization than pure licenses or hardware sales**.

In his 2015 shareholder letter, for the first time Satya started mentioning highlights which are focused on **cloud**, **usage** and **consumption**.[7]

Themes that you will see coming back are **commercial cloud** and **run rate**. In addition, Satya started to mention **ubiquitous computing** and **ambient intelligence**.

Moreover, this is the first time Microsoft describes the framework it uses to talk about digital transformation:

---

[7] From the 2015 shareholder letter: Commercial cloud annualized revenue run rate exceeded $12.1 billion, up more than 50 percent year-over-year. More than 70 million people use Office 365 commercial every single month. Revenue from, Azure, grew triple digits, with usage of key computing and database workloads more than doubling year-over-year. Windows 10 is now active on more than 400 million devices around the world and over 197 billion hours of usage. This is the fastest adoption rate of any prior Windows release. Bing has leveraged this incredible usage to become profitable with search advertising revenue up 17 percent. Xbox Live monthly active users grew 33 percent year-over-year to 49 million.

engaging customers, empowering employees, optimizing operations and transforming products.

The 2017 fiscal year was a year of consolidation and refinement. The most important change was Microsoft expanding its artificial intelligence (AI) efforts with creation of new Microsoft AI and Research Group in September 2016.[8]

Microsoft´s Paradigm Shift
July 2017

Since 2014 Satya Nadella had been talking about The Mobile first, Cloud first world. At Inspire 2017 Microsoft

---

[8] Edited excerpts from the press release: Microsoft has formed the Microsoft AI and Research Group, bringing together Microsoft's world-class research organization with more than **5,000** computer scientists and engineers focused on the company's AI product efforts. **Microsoft is dedicated to democratizing AI for every person and organization, making it more accessible and valuable to everyone and ultimately enabling new ways to solve some of society's toughest challenges.** Today's announcement builds on the company's deep focus on AI and will accelerate the **delivery of new capabilities to customers across agents, apps, services and infrastructure. Microsoft is taking a four-pronged approach** to its initiative to democratize AI: **Agents.** Harness AI to fundamentally change human and computer interaction through agents such as Microsoft's digital personal assistant Cortana.
Applications. Infuse every application with intelligence. **Services.** Make these same intelligent capabilities that are infused in Microsoft's apps —cognitive capabilities such as vision and speech, and machine analytics — available to every application developer in the world. **Infrastructure.** Build the world's most powerful AI supercomputer with Azure and make it available to anyone, to enable people and organizations to harness its power.

shifted the paradigm to the Intelligent cloud and the Intelligent edge and at the same time increased their total addressable market to 4.5T$.[9]

Edited excerpts from Satya Nadella´s speech at Inspire:

"This intelligent cloud and intelligent edge era is going to be defined by **three key characteristics**. The first is that **every experience** that you build is going to be **multi-device and multi-sense**."

"The **second profound shift** is the **infusion** of **AI**."

"To manage all of this complexity we need a new efficient frontier for how we develop applications, distribute applications, manage applications. That's what the **server-less revolution** is all about, containers, micro-services, server-less, these are technologies that are going to be more profound than virtualization ever was."

Windows becoming the Edge of the Cloud:

In March 2018 Satya made one of the most important statements on the future of Microsoft.[10] The Windows and Devices group ceased to exist, and Windows engineering was broken up into the O365 Engineering group and the Cloud & Enterprise Engineering group.

---

[9] Inspire is the new name for the Microsoft worldwide partner conference or WPC. This gathering happens each July and around 15.000 people from the partner community come together to hear the latest on Microsoft strategy, products and to network with Microsoft employees and other partners.

[10] https://news.microsoft.com/2018/03/29/satya-nadella-email-to-employees-embracing-our-future-intelligent-cloud-and-intelligent-edge/

Windows is becoming more of a supporting platform for the cloud.

Some of these signals could already be seen. The creation of Microsoft365 in July 2017 already signaled that Microsoft was using the strength of O365 to pull through Windows. [11]

The Cloud and Enterprise engineering team under Scott Guthrie became the Cloud and AI platform team.

The Four Platforms

During the Build conference in May 2018 Satya went deeper on the new worldview by focusing on the advances in intelligent edge.[12]

An interesting evolution is that not only Microsoft´s mission is aligned to empower others, Nadella now also closely aligns the success of customers to Microsoft´s success via its products and business model. "We are focused on building technology so that we can empower others to build more technology. We have aligned our mission -empower every person and every organization on the planet to achieve more - the products we build and our business model so that your success is what leads to our success. There has to be complete alignment."

Nadella does this against on the one hand a backdrop against how Facebook and Google are using customer

---

[11] Microsoft started pulling EMS, Enterprise Mobility and Security, itself a suite of separate products, into O365 first with the Secure Productive Enterprise offering, using the O365 strength to sell EMS. Now Microsoft added Windows 10 to this with Microsoft365.

[12] Build is Microsoft´s annual developer conference

data as a main driver of their business model and on the other hand against AWS, with Amazon competing more directly with entire industries.

Beyond the Cloud

Satya has given us a glimpse of where Microsoft is heading in the future in his book Hit Refresh. Microsoft is looking at its investment strategy from a ´three horizons´ perspective. The first horizon is about growing today´s core business and technologies; the second about incubating new products and ideas for the future; and the third is about investing in long-term break-troughs.

Horizon one entails quarter-by-quarter, year-by-year innovations in all of Microsoft´s businesses. Horizon two includes some nearer-term platform shifts, such as new user interfaces with speech or digital ink, new applications with personal assistants and bots, and Internet of Things experiences for everything from factories to cars to home appliances. However, it is horizon three where Microsoft is placing big bets: Mixed reality, artificial intelligence and quantum computing. [13]

---

[13] Hit Refresh chapter 6: "With mixed reality we are building the ultimate computing experience, one in which your field of view becomes a computing surface and the digital world, and your physical world become one. Artificial intelligence powers every experience, augmenting human capability with insights and predictive power that would be impossible to achieve on our own. Finally, quantum computing will allow us to go beyond the bounds of Moore's Law by changing the very physics of computing as we know it today, providing the computational power to solve the world's biggest and most complex problems.

Conclusions

Satya Nadella started his vision for Microsoft with a ten-page document that he created for the board during thanksgiving in 2013. [14]

In that document, he refers to more ubiquitous computing, ambient intelligence, cloud and edge computing. Things you see come back later in Microsoft´s mission, vision, strategy, business models and products.

For the author the focus over the next couple of years is on Cloud, Big Data and AI. Mixed Reality will remain more of a niche and Quantum Computing is a search for the Holy Grail with a large payback for those who get there first. In order to do AI you need to have your data estate in order and the cloud facilitates this.

Lessons for Partners

To understand where Microsoft is going do your homework. Study and read what Nadella says as this will give you a view a couple of years out.

Cloud is still important and is going hybrid. But the next big thing is AI. The AI tidal wave will pull through a lot of data projects. Compute goes where the data is.

Invest in cloud yesterday, in big data and AI today. Mixed reality is still a niche. If you invest here, you are ahead of the general curve and only very specialized partners will make money in the short term.

MR, AI, and quantum may be independent threads today, but they are going to come together. We're betting on it."
[14] Hit Refresh Chapter 3.

Chapter 2. Microsoft´s Business Model

Microsoft describes what it offers to the market like this:

"We develop, license, and support a wide range of **software products, services, and devices** that deliver new opportunities, greater convenience, and enhanced value to people's lives."

"Our products include operating systems; cross-device productivity applications; server applications; business solution applications; desktop and server management tools; software development tools; video games; and training and certification of computer system integrators and developers. We also design, manufacture, and sell devices, including PCs, tablets, gaming and entertainment consoles, other intelligent devices, and related accessories that integrate with our cloud-based offerings. We offer an array of services, including cloud-based solutions that provide customers with software, services, platforms, and content, and we provide solution support and consulting services. We also deliver relevant online advertising to a global audience." [15]

---

[15] From the 2017 10-K document http://view.officeapps.live.com/op/view.aspx?src=https://c.s-microsoft.com/en-us/CMSFiles/MSFT_FY17_10K.docx?version=c33e3c7b-17ce-cd84-7e64-217cc6253359

The Satya Era: All about Cloud & Services 2014-2017

Satya inherited a financial reporting structure that was not in line with his vision for Microsoft. Microsoft was still the Windows and Office Company. PC's sales had been falling for years as secular shifts to mobile computing ate into Microsoft's most profitable business model. AWS was the only serious player in cloud computing.

In all the three interconnected ambitions, it is about how fast Microsoft is moving to the cloud. In productivity and business processes, it is about Office 365, Dynamics 365 and LinkedIn. In the intelligent cloud platform, it is about Azure and even in the more personal computing segment Windows is moving to a as a service model and Microsoft is looking at extended ways to monetize Windows.

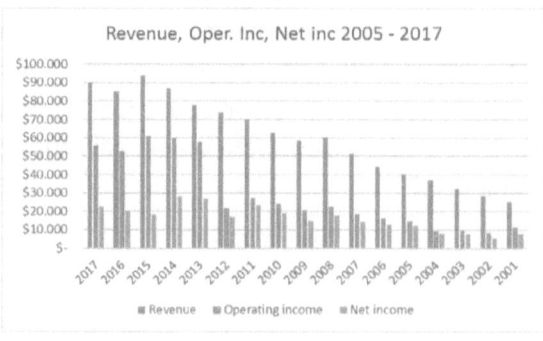

Figure 1: Microsoft Revenue, Operating Income and Net Income 2001-2017

Microsoft's reported run rate for its commercial cloud was $4.4B, $9.4B, $12.1B and $18.9B from 2014 to 2017. This makes Microsoft one of the biggest enterprise cloud players in the world. Microsoft generated about $5B of cloud revenue in 2017, which was 17 percent of the all up revenue. [16]

Cloud margins

Delivering cloud services has a lower gross margin than selling software as you must provide all the underlying infrastructure and services. Between the different segments, Productivity and Business processes (PBP) has a higher cloud margin than intelligent cloud (where Azure sits). As Azure is growing faster than PBP the gross margins will go down over time. Microsoft is compensating this via selling higher value Azure services. Then there is the scale component. At a certain level of scale, the cloud business gross margins tend to go up. [17]

The FY 2017 all up gross margin for Microsoft was 64 percent, the commercial cloud gross margin was an average of 50 percent over the four quarters.

Q4 2017 was the last time that Microsoft called out its annualized commercial cloud run rate. In Q1 2018 Microsoft started calling out commercial cloud revenue at $5.0B and states the FY2017 numbers per quarter at $3.2B, $3.4B, $3.8B and $4.5B respectively. This makes for a 56 percent growth over a rolling 12 months period.

---

[16] The Q4 2017 earnings call was the first time that Amy Hood mentioned the all up commercial cloud revenue. Until then Microsoft only spoke about run rate.
[17] This is what happened at Amazon with AWS which is now the biggest profit contributor to Amazon.

Quarter	Revenue B$	GM%	12Months growth
FY17 Q1	3,2	49%	
FY17Q2	3,4	48%	
FY17Q3	3,8	51%	
FY17Q4	4,5	52%	
FY18Q1	5	57%	56,3%
FY18Q2	5,3	55%	55,9%
FY18Q3	6	57%	57,9%

Table 1. Microsoft Cloud Revenue

It is interesting to notice that the Microsoft cloud properties and AWS are similar in size and growing at the same rate.[18] Microsoft also seems to be doing a good job of increasing the cloud margins.

Conclusions

Of the three business segments, Productivity and Business Processes, Intelligent Cloud segment and More Personal Computing, the biggest revenue contributor is still More Personal Computing, then Productivity and Business Processes, and then Intelligent Cloud.

More Personal Computing is in a down market that will go down structurally. In Productivity and Business Processes Microsoft is converting on premise-installed base to the

---

[18] Although all of Amazons growth is accretive. Part of Microsoft´s cloud growth is cannibalizing on premise business.

cloud.[19] Intelligent Cloud is where the real battle for market share happens.

Simplifying Microsoft's strategic imperatives: Microsoft needs to protect, as long as possible, the more personal computing segment. Strategically Microsoft now has gravitated towards O365 as a pull for Windows by creating Microsoft365. Microsoft needs to convert the Office installed base as quickly as possible to the cloud to defend its market share from others like Google and Slack. Microsoft still has a large addressable market in the SMB space for O365.[20]

However, the real battle for new market share is in the Azure space. That is where for the last couple of years the focus of Microsoft has been, Azure, Azure and Azure. Microsoft must do this against a backdrop of decreasing gross margin percentage due to a higher cloud mix, which has a lower gross margin percentage than selling software licenses although there is now an upward trend in cloud gross margins.

Lessons for Partners

Microsoft is all about the cloud now but there are different clouds and depending on how much help

---

[19] Amy Hood made an interesting comment during the presentation of the FY 17 results; "for the first time, Office 365 Commercial revenue surpassed revenue from our traditional licensing business."

[20] Bitglass in a 2018 study on cloud puts the O365 penetration in companies under 500 employee at 49.6 percent versus over 73 percent for companies above 500 employees. https://pages.bitglass.com/FY18BR-CloudAdoption_LP.html

Microsoft needs, you will feel a different level of interest from Microsoft.

With O365 Microsoft is the clear market leader and Microsoft feels that it doesn´t need a lot of help.[21] The large white space is in SMB but if you only focus on O365 you will not get a lot of attention from Microsoft. If you focus on Microsoft365 you will get a bit more attention as it is the new SKU that they want to make successful. [22]

Dynamics365 is relatively new. Microsoft has many Dynamics partners that know the on-premise world but not a lot that know the cloud world very well. As a long-term Dynamics partner you need to convert to cloud now. There is also an interesting opportunity for new partners to get into this business due to the increased integration of Dynamics365 and O365.

Azure is THE cloud and Azure is where the big battle happens for Microsoft. Here there are different strategies and workloads. Microsoft is still very interested in getting customers that are not using Azure to use Azure. However, more and more you will see Microsoft pushing higher value add Azure services like Media Services, Data & Analytics, Enterprise Integration, IOT and AI & Cognitive services instead of compute, networking and storage. As a partner, you must move beyond the basic Azure workloads.

---

[21] Research done by Bitglass on cloud adoption of 135.00 companies has O365 adoption going from 7,7% in 2014 to 34,3% in 2016 to 56,3% in 2018. https://pages.bitglass.com/FY18BR-CloudAdoption_LP.html

[22] SKU is Stock Keeping Unit, in general used to describe a product reference.

Cloud also means consumption so as a partner you will need to have a clear strategy on how you drive consumption of Microsoft cloud services in your accounts.

24

Chapter 3. Co-opetition

In this chapter, we will discuss both Microsoft´s competition and how Microsoft competes. We will also look at some of the partnering strategies.

How competing has changed under Nadella

Since Nadella has taken over Microsoft is seen as more eco-system and partner friendly and less openly aggressive than during the Gates and Ballmer times.

In Hit Refresh Nadella dedicates an entire chapter to building partnerships. The following excerpts will help the reader understand how Nadella thinks about partnerships.

"Today one of my top priorities is to make sure that our billion customers, no matter which phone or platform they choose to use, have their needs met so that we continue to grow. To do that, sometimes we have to bury the hatchet with old rivals, pursue surprising new partnerships, and revive longstanding relationships. Over the years we've developed the maturity to become more obsessed with customer needs, thereby learning to coexist and compete. Healthy partnerships—often difficult but always mutually beneficial—are the natural and much-needed product of the culture we're building."

"Partnering is too often seen as a zero-sum game—whatever is gained by one participant is lost by another. I don't see it that way. When done right, partnering grows the pie for everyone—for customers, yes, but also for each of the partners."

"In today's era of digital transformation, every organization and every industry are potential partners. Companies are focused on ensuring that they stay relevant and competitive by embracing this transformation and we want Microsoft to be their partner."

Competing in the cloud world

To compete in the cloud world with your own cloud you need tremendous resources. Only a few companies have the money to be able to invest between five and ten billion dollars a year in scaling out datacenters.[23] AWS can do this as it was a first mover, captured a lot of market share and is a cash rich company.[24] Microsoft has the deep pockets. Google has. It is our expectation that there will be a couple of hyper scale cloud providers and Microsoft will certainly be one of them.[25]

---

[23] An excellent article that analyses the capex investment in datacenters by Google, AWS and Microsoft can be found here: http://www.platformonomics.com/2017/04/follow-the-capex-cloud-table-stakes/

[24] Amazon points to something it calls the "virtuous cycle" that has helped drive the cloud industry. The more customers a cloud platform provider signs up, the more servers it can afford to add. The more servers it has, the better it can take advantage of economies of scale and offer customers lower prices for more robust features, including ones likely to appeal to enterprises. The lower the prices and the better the products, the more customers the provider will likely attract — and the more new customers will switch over to the cloud.

[25] Our view is that the hyperscale cloud providers will be Amazon, Microsoft, Google, Alibaba, Tencent, Huawei and maybe one day Facebook and Apple.

In IaaS Microsoft is competing with AWS, Hosters and Telco's. In SaaS with Salesforce and other app providers. In PaaS with Google, AWS and Salesforce.[26] In our estimation, AWS is currently three times the size of Azure although Azure is catching up.[27] For Microsoft Azure is where the real battle happens. Microsoft has been successful in defending the Office franchise with O365 growing over 50% over the last couple of years, more than compensating for the decline of on premise Office licenses. Azure is where Microsoft needs to capture market share.

Microsoft´s differentiator versus Amazon is hybrid. That is in our opinion why Satya has changed the paradigm from Cloud First, Mobile First to the Intelligent Cloud and the Intelligent Edge. Hybrid comes in different shapes. First hybrid means that all Microsoft technology has the same code base and therefore Microsoft´s cloud is easy extensible to on premise. Microsoft has released Azure stack, which enables customers and partners to create their own Azure cloud on premise which can be extended with public Azure services.

Furthermore, Microsoft want to be the most trusted and secure cloud, which is respectful of data privacy and location. Google and AWS are very much public cloud oriented.

The hybrid approach will also extend the lifetime of the assets of Hosters, Outsourcers and Telco's. They can extend their own data center assets into the Azure cloud.

---

[26] Force.com

[27] AWS is on a trajectory to be around $22-24B in 2018. Microsoft never gives out Azure only revenue numbers. In the Q3 2017 quarterly earnings release call during Q&A Goldman Sachs estimated Azure to be on $8B annualized revenue.

That way they can offer increased security, privacy and control to customers in public sector or industries that do not or cannot have some of their data in the public cloud while at the same time offering the flexibility and extensibility of the Azure public cloud for other services for these same customers. Microsoft is less of an enemy to the Hosters, Outsourcers and Telco´s than AWS or Google are.

Competing in the AI world

Satya was asked the following question at the Morgan Stanley Technology, Media & Telecom Conference on February 26, 2018: "In terms of Microsoft and your capabilities, how are you guiding Microsoft to ensure that you're in the running, that you're the vendor that your customers are looking toward when they're thinking about machine-learning, when they think about cognitive services, that they should be coming to your platform versus other big competitors out there?"

Satya gives a two-pronged answer. "First, of course you have to have the technology." He refers to Microsoft and maybe two to three other companies out there having Ai capabilities. [28] Secondly, he states: "The question that every customer, whether it's a financial services company, whether it's a retailer, whether it is a manufacturer is going to ask is, who do I trust, especially in a world where there's going to be transfer learning?"

"I think that's where having this purity of business model which we have which is fundamentally consumption-based or subscription-based, not having all these funky

---

[28] We guess he refers to Google, AWS, IBM and maybe Alibaba.

cross-subsidies and marketplace structures and multiple businesses that on one side you compete and on the other side you partner. I just think most people are going to see through it."

He takes a stab at Amazon here. Amazon can become your competition. Microsoft will be the platform company that democratizes AI and that you will pay for using its platform and that you can trust with your data. [29]

Conclusions.

Microsoft has moved from being (seen as) a monopoly, having anti-competitive practices, bundling products, Wintel, Linux is a cancer, Ballmer laughing at iPhone[30] and pushing Windows and Office to a company that integrates open source, has its most important battle as the runner up (Azure) and all of that with a newly found style thanks to Nadella. From competitive winner takes all to co-operative.

Lessons for Partners

Satya has brought clarity in the compete model by clearly reaffirming that Microsoft is a platform company. This means a certain purity of business model. Microsoft is not going to be a retail company, nor a bank, nor a vertically specialized company competing with sector specific business solutions, nor are they going to sell your data to advertisers, nor are they going to use AI based on your

---

[29] Satya confirms this approach during a May 7th 2018 interview with CNBC https://www.cnbc.com/2018/05/07/microsofts-satya-nadella-trust-will-push-us-past-amazon-google.html
[30] https://www.youtube.com/watch?v=eywi0h_Y5_U

aggregate data to learn how to better perform your core business like some other competitors out there might do. As a partner, this is a key advantage in positioning the Microsoft platform and your services versus other providers in specific sectors. [31]

Microsoft is going to provide the platform for others to use and build upon and the customer will pay for that platform through a usage model.

However, that platform is adding functionality all the time. If you are a horizontal IP provider try to understand if Microsoft will one day integrate similar functionality into their platforms and run you out of business.

Microsoft is a lot more open to all the different technologies out there and embraces open source. This means that as a Microsoft partner you will need to start opening up to other technologies as well. As long as it runs on Azure Microsoft will love it.

Another important aspect of competition for partners is that in the future competition will come from abroad through the increased acceptance of app stores and the focus of Microsoft on repeatable IP. This at the same time also opens up a wider market for partners.

---

[31] There are multiple references of large retail companies that have banned AWS as a platform.

Chapter 4. The Microsoft Culture

In this chapter we want to give a feeling for the Microsoft culture and the impact that Nadella is having on that culture so that you, as a partner, can understand how best to engage with Microsoft.

The Nadella Effect

To Nadella, culture is critical. [32] You will see and hear him speak about culture, soul and other 'soft' areas a lot. That already is a big change from his predecessors. He dedicates a whole chapter to culture in Hit Refresh. [33] Nadella: "The CEO is the curator of an organization's culture. Anything is possible for a company when its culture is about listening, learning, and harnessing individual passions and talents to the company's mission. Creating that kind of culture is my chief job as CEO."

Nadella and Microsoft have embraced the work of Carol Dweck, a psychology professor at Stanford, around

---

[32] USA Today Microsoft CEO Nadella: 'Culture is everything' and Microsoft's Satya Nadella is counting on culture shock to drive growth
https://eu.usatoday.com/story/tech/2015/09/15/microsoft-ceo-nadella-culture-everything/72330296/ and https://www.usatoday.com/story/tech/news/2017/02/20/microsofts-satya-nadella-counting-culture-shock-drive-growth/98011388/

[33] Hit Refresh Chapter 4 A Cultural Renaissance. From Know-It-Alls to Learn-It-All's

growth mindsets.[34] People who view talent as a quality they either possess or lack have a "fixed mindset." People with a "growth mindset", in contrast, enjoy challenges, strive to learn, and consistently see potential to develop new skills.[35]

Nadella states that the culture change he wanted was rooted in the Microsoft he originally joined and is centered on exercising a growth mindset every day in three distinct ways. Obsess about customers, actively seek diversity and inclusion and be one company and not a confederation of fiefdoms.

Nadella admits in his book that it is hard to drive a culture change across such a large organization and reflects on how Microsoft has not done a good enough job to get middle managers involved in this culture change.

Nadella has three leadership principles for anyone leading others at Microsoft:

"The first is to bring clarity to those you work with. This is one of the foundational things leaders do every day, every minute. In order to bring clarity, you've got to synthesize the complex. Leaders take internal and external noise and synthesize a message from it, recognizing the true signal within a lot of noise. I don't want to hear that someone is the smartest person in the room. I want to hear them take their intelligence and use it to develop deep shared

---

[34] https://www.amazon.com/Mindset-Psychology-Carol-S-Dweck/dp/0345472322/ref=sr_1_1?ie=UTF8&qid=1525245401&sr=8-1&keywords=carol+dweck
[35] https://hbr.org/2014/11/how-companies-can-profit-from-a-growth-mindset and https://hbr.org/2016/01/what-having-a-growth-mindset-actually-means

understanding within teams and define a course of action."

"Second, leaders generate energy, not only on their own teams but across the company. It's insufficient to focus exclusively on your own unit. Leaders need to inspire optimism, creativity, shared commitment, and growth through times good and bad. They create an environment where everyone can do his or her best work. And they build organizations and teams that are stronger tomorrow than today."

"Third, and finally, they find a way to deliver success, to make things happen. This means driving innovations that people love and are inspired to work on; finding balance between long-term success and short-term wins; and being boundary-less and globally minded in seeking solutions."

Conclusions

Microsoft is on a path to a culture change driven by Nadella that is about being open, inclusive and focused on a growth mindset. Key external examples of that can been seen since Nadella took over leading to a completely different outside view of Microsoft. Internally however Microsoft comes from several decades of a culture honed by Gates and Ballmer which was extremely focused on outcomes, being smart, prepared, having all the answers and playing politics. This is changing, however culture change in a company of the size of Microsoft is not an easy and quick process.

Lessons for Partners

Microsoft employees are very busy as there is a lot of bureaucratic overhead involved working in a multinational company and specifically within Microsoft. They have to focus on customers and partners but have a lot of internal reporting to do. Don't waste their time. Be concise in what you want.

No matter how big or important you think you are many Microsoft employees assume that what is good for Microsoft is good for you. Keep that in mind when they announce the next big program or campaign. Evaluate it on the merits for you.

Understand the scorecard of the Microsoft organization and the people you work with and try to find win-wins.

Chapter 5. How Microsoft organizes.

In this chapter we will look at the Microsoft organization not only from the physical organization angle but also at how Microsoft organizes through its ´Rhythm of Business´ and we will discuss the field organization and its impact on engaging with partners.

Microsoft´s strategy process.

Although Microsoft starts its fiscal year in July, we would like to start to explain the overall strategy process by starting in January. In January, Microsoft starts its MYR or Mid-Year Review. Starting with the corporate organizations first, senior execs helped by their staff go through the performance of every organization in excruciating detail. Then they reconvene, draw general conclusions and then it is up to the geographical areas to do the same to each country.

Then it is up to corporate to review the area performance. The whole process finishes by mid-February. This process is extremely time consuming, but Microsoft is one of the very few companies in the world that has this level of detail on their operations.

The strategy teams in corp then go off and do their work until early April when the PRISM meetings start (Priority setting meetings). These meetings are for senior execs, country managers and M&O leads. This is where Microsoft explains the strategy and expected execution for next fiscal year starting in July. This is then documented in detailed WWSMM memos (World Wide Subsidiary Marketing Memo) and detailed organizational and role blueprints. April, May and June are also the time when budgets are negotiated.

Microsoft is a very top down driven organization and, in the field, very homogeneous. Due to its structure and systems of management control, Microsoft is capable of completely changing the direction of the company globally just in a couple of months and in worst case within a year. Very few large multi nationals have that capability.

Once the strategy is set, roles are defined, and budgets are negotiated Microsoft then, in July, starts communicating this to the global partner and sales community during Inspire and Ready[36].

Historically this has meant that Microsoft's Q4, April – June, was extremely busy for Microsoft employees. This is the last quarter of the fiscal year where sometimes more than 40 percent of the yearly number needed to be made.[37]

It is also the quarter when all planning happens. The skewing of revenue into Q4 will slowly change with the advent of cloud as you cannot wait to sell until the last quarter of the year.

---

[36] Ready was called MGX, Microsoft Global Exchange. This is the yearly event for Microsoft's sales teams which gathers about 15.00 people. In July 2018 Microsoft held Inspire and Ready at the same time which makes sense as a lot of the content and keynote speakers are the same. It is interesting that a company like Microsoft historically has explained its strategy to partners before explaining it to employees.

[37] With the month of June in some cases counting for 20 percent of yearly revenue.

The Microsoft organizational setup and the cloud world.

Microsoft´s sales model has been one of the most successful in the software world and that is at the same time the explanation of its limitation. The software model is based on selling pieces of technology to end customers´ IT organizations who then carry all the risk of making sure the development and deployment is successful. In addition, customers are paying upfront.

This model has changed with the advent of SaaS vendors who deliver end-to-end solutions to business users. In a cloud world, buyers buy more directly. The overall buying experience, marketing, onboarding support and continuous support to help drive that initial trial, sale, nurturing and usage are important.

The Commercial Sales Organization

In July 2017 Microsoft announced the biggest reorganization of their commercial sales model in the last ten years. The following are some of the changes.

- The corporate account segment (CAM-S) from within Small and Medium business (SMS&P) moves into the enterprise segment (EPG) creating a one enterprise commercial team.
- The Specialist Team Unit will be elevated to management board level reporting directly to the Country GM.
- A new unit called Customer Success is created with a direct reporting line to the country GM.
- A focus on industry within commercial Enterprise and some creation of first party (Microsoft

owned) vertical IP. Microsoft is focusing on six industries initially. Manufacturing & Resources, Financial Services, Retail, Government, Health & Education. These are the 'go big' industries where there is an agreement from the engineering teams to build 'light weight' IP. There is a set of additional emerging industries Microsoft will continue to look at.

- Integration of all separate partner organizations into a One Commercial Partner organization.
- Organizing all the field horizontal sales and consulting organization into four workloads: Modern Workplace, Business Applications, Apps & Infrastructure, Data & AI.

Customer Segmentation

Microsoft has moved from six customer segments to four, creating an enterprise sales motion in Enterprise and a scale sales motion in SMC, Small Medium and Corporate.

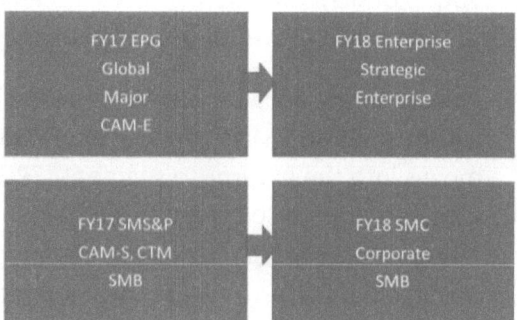

Figure 2. Microsoft FY18 Customer Segmentation (reproduced by the author).

The STU (Specialist Team Unit) has been elevated and a new CSU, customer success unit has been created reporting into the country manager. Most of the Account Team Units (ATU´s) are industry aligned if size permits.

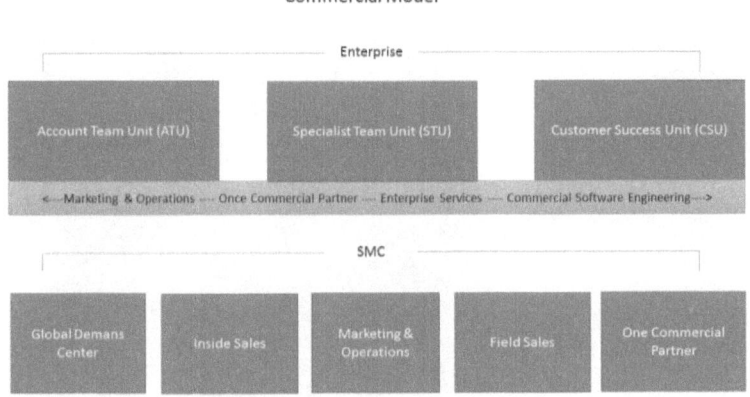

Figure 3. Microsoft´s FY18 Commercial model. (reproduced by the author).

The Specialist team Unit and the Customer Success Unit are aligned to the four solution areas, Modern workplace, Business applications, Apps and infrastructure and Data and AI. Microsoft claims that these solution areas are more aligned to the way customers buy. Compensation is aligned along these solution areas.

The One Commercial Partner Organization

Microsoft has split the partner engagement up in to three distinct groups that support a build with, Go to Market and Sell with motion.

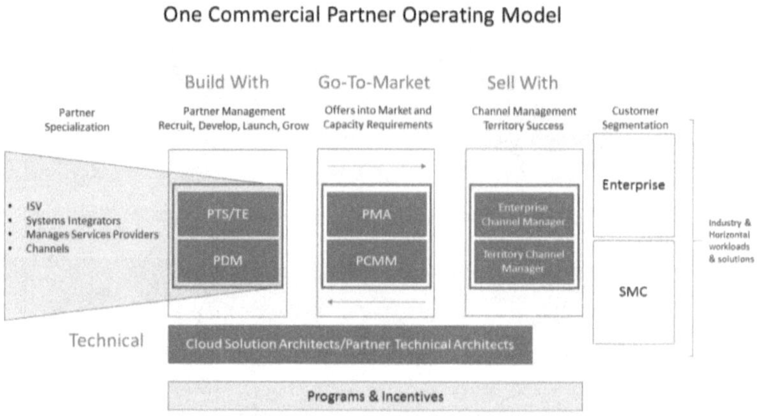

One Commercial Partner Operating Model

[Diagram: Build With — Partner Management (Recruit, Develop, Launch, Grow): PTS/TE, PDM. Go-To-Market — Offers into Market and Capacity Requirements: PMA, PCMM. Sell With — Channel Management Territory Success: Enterprise Channel Manager, Territory Channel Manager. Customer Segmentation: Enterprise, SMC. Partner Specialization: ISV, Systems Integrators, Manages Services Providers, Channels. Industry & Horizontal workloads & solutions. Technical: Cloud Solution Architects/Partner Technical Architects. Programs & Incentives.]

Figure 4. Microsoft´s One Commercial Partner Operating Model (reproduced by the author).

Build-with

The build with team works with the partners to develop new practices, new capabilities and new solutions. Managed partners will have a single point of contact (SPOC) in this team to help with building IP, partner transformation and growth plans. (Not a SPOC that will help with everything within Microsoft)

Sell-with.

Microsoft has concluded that partners want to work with Microsoft people that have a deep understanding of the accounts, that know the customers and that know the opportunities. The Enterprise channel managers and territory channel managers will fulfill this role.

The enterprise channel managers are aligned by industries and accounts. This means that, on the sell-with side, a partner will have to engage with multiple contacts versus a single point of contact on the build with side.

So, there is a SPOC on the left-hand side but multiple Microsoft people to engage with on the right-hand side, but the relevance and impact of these interactions should be higher.

Go-To-Market

The Go to Market people will help the partner define a demand generation strategy. The GTM piece is designed to help partners expand their demand generation engine and will be complemented with inside sales support.

Conclusions

This was a big reorganization for Microsoft which was well thought out on paper, but the implementation has its challenges. An additional challenge is that this model will work for partners that know Microsoft well but will be challenging for partners that do not have that deep knowledge of Microsoft and that needed a single point of contact to educate them and get them connected.

There will not be major changes in FY19 but just some minor tweaks. Some of the areas for improvement on which Microsoft will focus in our opinion:

- Solutions catalogue: how does Microsoft go from having a passive list of partner solutions to success in (re) selling these solutions?
- Cross border collaboration. There is very little incentive for Microsoft employees to help partners across borders but, most of all, little knowledge on how to do this.
- ISV engagement. With the disappeared DX organization there has been a lot less focus on ISVs in the field.
- Refinement of roles, or who does what. Expect there to be more clarity on what a PDM does versus what a channel manager does.
- Continued roll out of tele sales capabilities with the remaining field resources more and more focused on the enterprise accounts.

Lessons for partners

FY18 was a transition year. Long-term partners that know Microsoft well have survived the turmoil, as they are relatively independent. Partners that have less of a connection with Microsoft have struggled.

As a partner, you need to be pro-active towards Microsoft. You need to understand the organization, you need to understand who is who. There is no longer anybody who cares about your all up business within Microsoft. The onus of doing business on the Microsoft platform and with Microsoft is clearly on you.

Chapter 6. The Microsoft Partner Strategy

Introduction

You will hear Microsoft executives often state numbers about the partner ecosystem.[38] The most repeated number over the years is that 95 percent of Microsoft business is conducted via partners. This is an overstatement. A large part of the enterprise business is a result of Microsoft direct sales effort but is transacted via resellers.

Another often-used number is that for every dollar of Microsoft revenue the partner eco-system generates nine dollars.[39] Keep in mind that this is hardware revenue, software resale revenue and services revenue and includes the full end to end ecosystem that can be involved from getting software from Microsoft into a working project at a customer.

---

[38] At Inspire the following numbers where mentioned: Fore every $1 of Microsoft revenue, the partner ecosystem generates $9.01 - +6.600 new partners per month – 30 percent of partners joined the Microsoft Partner Network in the last twelve months – 17M people employed by partners around the globe – 95% of commercial revenue comes from partners – 64k+ cloud partners – more cloud partners than AWS, Google and Salesforce combined – Partners receive 19% higher margins than the next closest competitor.
[39] IDC Microsoft Footprint Model 2017.

A unique partner sales model
Microsoft has a different partner sales model compared to other software and cloud vendors. Most software vendors in the on premise world allowed services partners to resell with margins sometimes up to 50 percent on the software resold plus a large chunk of the yearly maintenance fees.[40]

The disadvantage of the three-year software renewal model and the fact that almost any company in the world is already a Microsoft customer is that if you are a services partner you are either involved before the license transaction when you are generating the opportunity or after when the needed software needs to deployed. This has been one of the main issues for Microsoft in measuring non-transactional partner performance and similarly measuring their internal teams that are working with these non-transactional partners.

Different partner types
Microsoft has been putting partners into boxes for years and organized the partner support roles along those boxes. You were either a License Solution Provider, a Distributor, a Solution partner, a Hoster, a Global Alliance, a Dynamics partner, an ISV, etc. Based on where you fit

---

[40] Microsoft only knew this model in the Dynamics space where it was an inherited way of doing business after buying Great Plains and Damgaard and stayed that way for a long time until the Dynamics organization was integrated into the overall partner motions as of FY15.

you got different incentives, different Microsoft people to work with, different programs to support you etc. [41]

Pre-Cloud partner Business models

Table 2 provides an overview of the different partner business models.

---

[41] Most of these partner classifications do not need an explanation except for the License Solution Provider. Most of Microsoft's commercial enterprise software sales are transacted through LSP's or Licensing Solution Partners (LSP's were known as LAR's or Large Account Resellers until July 2013). An LSP has the contractual engagement with the customer and handles any yearly true ups, licensing renewals, software asset management and is the extended admin arm of Microsoft. The advantage of being an LSP is that you have detailed knowledge of all the software that a customer uses. However, LSP's tend to resell Microsoft licenses with an average margin of 3% or less and they incur the payment risk. It is a financial business. Microsoft has been reducing the amount of LSP's and has been helping a small set of LSP's become global players.

There are a couple of reasons Microsoft created the LSP's. It enabled Microsoft to outsource a lot of the administrative work. It helped offload the financial risk of non-paying customers and in specific parts of the world, it made it easier for Microsoft to assume all business was done by the local rules through the LSP and there was no need for Microsoft to get into the details.

Initially a lot of the LSP's business was referred to the LSP's by Microsoft. Microsoft has created a dependency on LSP's as LSP's can be instrumental in quarter ends and make or break a quarter which gives them a lot of negotiating power with the Microsoft field. This however is changing with more and more cloud business instead of on premise licenses.

Partner Type	Business Model	End Customer engagement level	What Microsoft likes about partner	What Microsoft doesn't like about partner	What partner likes about Microsoft	What partner doesn't like about Microsoft
Software Reseller/ LSP	High volume, transactional and administrative excellence	Procurement, CIO, -1, -2.	Reach, scale and reduces financial and admin burden	Power of reseller at contract renewal stage	Microsoft provides leads. Privileged license positioning info and software usage understanding.	Very low margins on pure software transaction
Distributor	Resell of Hardware and software to other channel players	None. Directly with other channel participants	Capillarity, reach, financial muscle, marketing muscle.		Microsoft provided funding, rebates.	
Outsourcer and Managed services provider	Services model with positive ROI only later in the contract.	CIO and sometimes CFO, COO, CEO		Microsoft effectively is locked out of critical customer conversation. Reduced innovation	License mobility. End customer can transfer licenses to outsourcer.	Microsoft cloud ambitions are impacting business model
Hoster	Large upfront investment recouped through a recurring services model.	CIO, CIO -1, CIO -2	Scalable and very profitable business model.	Lack of transparency on license usage	Large installed base of customers. De facto standard technology	Hard to differentiate. Microsoft cloud ambitions are impacting business model
Telco	Very large upfront investment recouped through a recurring services model.	Enterprise, SMB, B2C. In B2B typically CIO -1, -2, Procurement, Facilities	Reach, scale	Very slow decision making		Potential competition for core business model
Systems Integrator	Project based services (mostly mixed with managed services as well)	CxO, LOB, CIO	Influencing capabilities and execution muscle	Hard to get consistent global traction	De facto standard at customers	No synchronized sales motion
ISV	High upfront investment in R&D, high sales cost, and high margin.	LOB, CIO, CxO	Creating network effects for Microsoft platform	Some ISVs are very entrenched with Microsoft competitors or are direct competitors	Microsoft cloud platform. Microsoft enterprise salesforce for co-sell motion	Sometimes Microsoft moves up the value chain competing with technology ISVs

49

OEM	High upfront investment, global scale and volume, low margins	Procurement, CIO -1, -2	Very profitable business model for Microsoft	Shipment of naked PC's.[95]	De facto PC standard	Lack of choice/options
Business Consultant	Project based services	CEO, CXO, LOB, CIO	Customer Access Level	Difficult to scale as all countries are limited liability partnerships	One of the global technology platforms, Cloud, AI, Big Data capabilities	Sees most Microsoft employees as too technical/not business oriented
Dynamics partner	Project based, software resell, software maintenance, IP, HW	LOB, CFO, CIO	Very Microsoft oriented. Customer access level	Late in adjusting to cloud world.	Software margins	Microsoft aggressively changing the business model to cloud.
Solution Partner	Project based services. Managed services, maintenance. Some IP.	CIO, CIO -1, -2. Innovation. Some LOB	Very Microsoft focused in general.		Good support from the Microsoft field. Deal investments.	
Learning partner	Selling training	HR, Training department, CIO -2	Helps in improving overall skill level of the market			Microsoft removing the learning competency.

Table 2. Partner business model overview

Microsoft has always done well with resellers, OEMs, solution partners and Dynamics partners. Microsoft did well with ISVs, then 'forgot' about them during a couple of years and now sees their importance again. Microsoft has had a mediocre engagement with larger systems integrators.[42] Microsoft has not had a good track record with outsourcers and Telco's.

---

[42] Not because of the overall strategy and execution with large system integrators at a global level but because of the lack and focus of investment at the field level.

Microsoft's partner strategy summarized

Microsoft's partner strategy can be summarized as follows:

- Give every partner the possibility to resell cloud services.
- Have partners create IP on the Microsoft platforms (Azure, Dynamics365 and O365) to make these platforms stickier and publish that IP in Microsoft app stores.
- Make sure that partners that have existing IP move to the Microsoft platform.
- Make sure partners are less generalist and more specialists.
- Move partners up the value chain so they talk to line of business and CxO
- Work with new types of partners that already have that CxO engagement

What should a partner do?

What does Microsoft say you should be doing? We will try to an answer that in table 3.

Partner Type	Cloud Impact	Microsoft Strategy Impact	Partner strategies
Software Reseller	High.	High.	Move aggressively to add project services and managed services to your portfolio. Become an indirect CSP provider.
Outsourcer and Managed services provider	High	Medium	Include the Microsoft platform into your offerings and offer a Hybrid solution. Move to outcome-based solutions.
Hoster	High	High	Try to integrate Hyperscale clouds into your offering. Hybrid offering through Microsoft Azure Stack.
Telco	High	Medium	Telco's are impacted by Apple, Facebook, Google, Netflix, Microsoft and all the messaging platforms. Integrate Hyperscale clouds into your offering. Build intelligent networks. Use your capillarity for reselling.
Systems Integrator	Medium	Medium	Specialize. Build IP. Resell via CSP. Become a managed services provider.
ISV	High	Low	Move your solutions aggressively to a cloud platform and cloud revenue model. Co-sell with Microsoft. P2P with the Microsoft channel.
OEM	High	Low	Microsoft will try to protect OEMs as long as they can. With all the cloud services and mobile platforms, the replacement cycles of PC's will become longer. Strategies: become the biggest, innovate with design, milk the model as long as possible. Differentiate market segments.
Business Consultant	Medium	Low	Increase technical skills to get deep on cloud platforms. AI and Big Data are providing transformational consulting opportunities.
Dynamics partner	Medium	High	Adjust to a poorer incentive model from Microsoft. Aggressively move to Dynamics365. Add services and skills more down in the technology stack. Extend to O365, PowerBI, Flow, PowerApps and Azure. Specialize. Build managed services. Resell via CSP.
Solution Partner	Medium	Low	Solution partners need to move aggressively to selling and implementing cloud projects. Additional opportunity for making money by becoming a CSP. Specialize. Build IP. Resell via CSP. Become a managed services provider.
Learning Partner	Medium	High	Learning partners need to rethink their value add which most probably lies in specialization.

Table 3. Microsoft partner strategic options

Conclusions

The trends as described before mean that many of the existing partner business models are under threat from general market trends on the one hand and from Microsoft's strategy on the other hand.

There is a convergence of partner business models going on. All partners start to do all four core activities (IP creation, projects, managed services and resell) but they will gravitate differently across this spectrum. There is a big focus on creating differentiated IP. Cloud is commoditizing infrastructure and being asset heavy is not an advantage per se. Technology buying decisions are increasingly being taken by C-suite and LoB versus IT decision makers.

Ecosystems are being created and you need to understand strategically in which ones to play. Customers and other partners will buy via market places. Microsoft is driving end-to-end scenarios on increasingly wide and complex platforms.

Lessons for partners

Microsoft in general tells a partner where they want them to go, however very few people at Microsoft know what it takes as a partner to transform, as they have never driven a transformation themselves. The closest they can relate to a transformation is through Microsoft´s own transformation, which does not translate very well to most partner business models.

Chapter 7. Required knowledge to partner with Microsoft.

There are some things that you need to understand when partnering with Microsoft. What the Microsoft Partner Network is, what Microsoft competencies are, how Microsoft´s licensing works, how the Cloud Solution Provider (CSP) program works and how partner incentives work.

The Microsoft Partner Network.

You don't have to become a Microsoft partner if you want to use Microsoft technology in your solutions or if you implement Microsoft technologies at customers.

However, being a partner gives you access to incentives, marketing materials, training, presales support, tech support and internal use rights to Microsoft software.

There are three levels of partnership. Network member, Microsoft Action Pack and Competency partner which is the highest level. You can have silver competencies and/or gold competencies. A gold competency level is the highest status a partner can get.

As an action pack member, you get a limited number of licenses.[43] The number for competency partners is more

---

[43] https://assets.microsoft.com/es-es/mpn-maps-software-iur-license-table.pdf

generous. You can earn additional licenses based on selling or influencing Microsoft cloud services.[44]

Microsoft Competencies

A Microsoft competency is a stamp of approval that you, as a partner, have skills, capabilities and customer references in certain technology areas. There are six competency categories and eighteen individual competencies.

The categories are: Application development and ISV, Cloud Platform & Infra, Data Management & Analytics, Business Applications, Mobility and Productivity.

To get Microsoft competencies, you need to have individuals at your company pass certain exams, you need customer references and you need to pay the competency fees.

Microsoft does not change competencies often as getting to a competency status for a partner can be a journey of multiple years between training employees, passing exams and getting a minimum amount of customer references. You also need to requalify every year with new references otherwise you lose your competency.

As a partner if you want to play seriously in the Microsoft ecosystem you need to be a competency partner. To be a competency partner, you need to invest in training your

---

[44] For example Action Pack subscribers Partners can earn additional Office 365 licenses by selling Microsoft Online Services. Partners are eligible to receive an additional five seats of Office 365 after selling 25 seats of Office 365 within the previous 12 months.

people and you need to pay the fee every year. It is a cost of doing business with Microsoft.

Licensing [45]

You might think that everything is cloud these days only about 25% of Microsoft's revenue is in the cloud currently. Even in the cloud you have to understand licensing. Understanding licensing at least at a conceptual level is important as it can impact your business as a partner.

Selling licenses is only an option for LSP's and resellers. However now any partner can become a Cloud Solution Provider and resell certain cloud services.

Customers can buy Microsoft licenses and cloud services either via commercial licensing agreements, via a cloud solution provider or directly on the web. For Service Providers Microsoft has a pay-as-you-go model available.[46]

The key to understanding which licensing vehicle to choose depends on

- The size and type of an organization.
- The products that an organization wants to license.
- The way in which an organization wants to use those products.

---

[45] We will refrain from going into to licensing for Public sector, nonprofits and educational institutions.
[46] Called a SPLA license, Services Provider License Agreement.

At the most basic level, the Microsoft Commercial Licensing agreement models address organizations in the following main categories:

- Customers with 500 or more users or devices should use an Enterprise Agreement
- Customers with 250 and or customers with 500 or more users that do not want an enterprise agreement can buy a Microsoft Products and Services Agreement (MPSA) for online services, software, and Software Assurance (optional).
- Customers with less than 250 users or devices can buy Open Licenses.

Volume Licensing agreements

Volume Licensing has three important components: agreements or programs, enrollments and software assurance.

An agreement is a procurement contract. In the contract Microsoft and the customer agree on many things. It has information on processes like True-Up and defines the length of the contract, the payment, terms for additional product license acquisitions, subsequent orders and perpetual rights.

Enrollments are contracts about the ordering of software. The customer promises to buy a certain quantity of software and certain types of software. In return, the customer receives discount. Enrollments are a Microsoft way to push customers in a certain direction. Software Assurance (SA) is a kind of maintenance contract.

The Cloud Solution Provider Program

The Cloud Solution Provider program is a licensing vehicle that enables all Microsoft partners to resell Microsoft cloud services.

The reasons that Microsoft states for launching the program are providing the partners with end to end customer ownership, creating a recurring revenue opportunity for partners and creating upsell and cross sell opportunities for partners.[47]

As partners are being paid for actual customer usage it is a key vehicle for Microsoft to drive cloud consumption. Another reason Microsoft created the program is in our view a long-term plan to reduce the dependency on volume licensing transactional partners.

Microsoft launched the program in FY15. The first workload on CSP was O365 which still accounts for about 80 percent of CSP revenue.[48] Later on, Microsoft added Azure, Dynamics, EMS and Windows Enterprise. You can now license from the desktop to the datacenter with CSP.

There are three different CSP models. A direct CSP, an indirect CSP reseller and an indirect CSP provider option.

Microsoft recently announced that it is going to apply minimum volume requirements to direct CSP's and in

---

[47] https://assets.microsoft.com/en-us/IDC-partner-choice-for-cloud-success.pdf

[48] From two interviews with William Lewallen, Senior Manager for National Cloud Partner sales in Microsoft North America's Partner Business. Vince Menzione the ultimate guide to partnering. Episode 5 and 28
https://ultimateguidetopartnering.com/

their FY19 incentives the CSP direct incentives are similar to the CSP indirect reseller incentives. The only advantage of being CSP Direct is now the direct billing relationship with the customer.

In our view Microsoft is trying to reduce the amount of direct CSP´s. Most will become indirect resellers, some might become an indirect CSP provider if they can meet certain minimum volume requirements.

This is typical Microsoft. They first launch a program to go as broad as possible and to get as many partners in the program. Then they refine or redesign the program. In the agreement you sign to become part of the MPN, Microsoft clearly states that is has the right to cancel or change any program with a 30-day notice although they will try to give at least 90 days' notice.[49]

Reselling plain vanilla Microsoft Cloud Services will put you in competition with the whole world including Microsoft. You need an additional value proposition which can include additional managed services, additional IP, access to a very specific customer segment where you have a privileged position, etc.

---

[49] From the Microsoft partner Network Agreement: Changes to MPN Programs or Offers. Microsoft may update, change or remove any portion of an MPN Program or Offer, including incentives, campaigns, and programs, and Microsoft may cancel an entire MPN Program or Offer. Microsoft will use commercially reasonable efforts to provide you with 30 days' notice of such update or change, and 90 days' notice of any cancellation of an MPN Program or Offer. Your continued participation in an MPN Program or Offer following an update or change confirms your acceptance of such update or change. https://partners.microsoft.com/PartnerProgram/agreementprintable.aspx

Also, for a lot of partners moving into a subscription based, monthly model where you must do transactional billing and manage credit is very different from their core business. The CSP business is a monthly business that has its own metrics versus classic licensing like month over month growth versus year over year, customers and user versus contracts and revenue per customer and not contract value. Going into the CSP business as a direct CSP requires different skills in operations, sales, marketing and support.

Channel incentives [50]

Microsoft spends several billions of dollars on channel incentives each year. Five years ago, all channel incentives went to on premise software and almost all of it went to distributors and LSP´s. Nowadays 60 percent is going to cloud workloads and to a broader spectrum of partners via mechanisms like CSP.[51]

Microsoft incentives can be broadly seen in four categories.

- Enterprise incentives. This is where Microsoft wants to secure and maintain annuity relationships and drive cloud transformation and where partners can earn money for selling and transacting via EA or CSP.

---

[50] See a detailed overview of all Microsoft channel incentives at www.aka.ms/partnerincentives

[51] Microsoft states that the percentage of overall incentives going to cloud have evolved from 13% in FY13, 19% in FY14, 32% in FY15, 44% in FY16, to more than 50% in FY 17 and a planned more than 60% in FY18.

- SMB incentives. This is where Microsoft wants to expand partner and customer reach and frequency to drive cloud-based offerings and where partners can earn money for selling and transacting via Open licenses or CSP.
- Cloud services. This is where Microsoft wants to accelerate customer adoption, usage and consumption of online services across enterprise and SMB and partners can earn money via selling, deploying and managing online services solutions through any business model.
- Devices. Distributors and resellers can earn incentives by selling strategic devices like surface hub.

Conclusions

There is a level of investment you need to do in working with Microsoft as a partner. You need to be an official partner, you need to have competencies and you need to pay your fees. Then there are certain things you need to understand, to understand why Microsoft does things in a certain way. However, once you do that investment there is a wealth of assets, information, training and incentives out there. But you will only get something out of it if you study it and try to get the most out of all these benefits.

Lessons for partners

Knowing which licenses and products your customer has bought is important. Sometimes as a partner you are competing with other vendors that use technology from Microsoft´s competitors. If you understand the customers Microsoft licensing estate, you might be able to help the customer understand that your Microsoft based solution is cheaper because of the licenses that s/he already owns or because it is only a step-up license etc.

Microsoft will never share the full detail in writing of the customer´s license estate as this goes against data privacy laws. However, in our experience Microsoft people will hint to what the customer owns. LSP´s have an advantage as they know exactly what the customer owns and when he needs to renew.

There are a couple of ways to understand where Microsoft is going strategically. One way is to study through various mechanisms Microsoft´s strategy as explained in chapter 1. Another way is to understand where Microsoft is spending its money on channel incentives long, medium and short term.

Now the dollars are going to cloud, to usage & consumption and to the CSP model. In order to get the most out of the incentives program you have to invest time to study the incentives and claim them. The incentive scheme is complex and there is a lot of administrative overhead involved.

Chapter 8. Working with Microsoft Consulting Services

The last time Microsoft reported headcount in the product support & consulting unit was 2015 and at the time there were 32.000 people. However probably close to 20.000 are in product support. That leaves 12.000 people in MCS selling and delivering digital advisory, consulting projects and premier support.

MCS tends to focus on larger customer engagements and intents to make the market for Microsoft on new technologies or 'bleeding edge' projects. However, MCS runs a P&L and is bound to the same KPI's as any systems integrator. They need to sell, have their people be busy and not lose money on fixed price projects.

The premier business, the proactive support business, is at least half of the business and is the business with the highest customer satisfaction and the lowest risk.

Microsoft has made several strategic and operational changes with MCS over the years. At a certain moment in time MCS created IP on their own, then that was abandoned and now they seem to be doing some of that again.

Premier and consulting delivery have been pulled together and verticalized and they now no longer report locally into the services lead but into global domains. At a local level remains sales which has both a vertical sales team and workload focused sales roles. Delivery also has vertical managers who report up to a delivery manager and reporting into these vertical managers are account delivery executives.

MCS is expensive and they have very high rates compared to any Microsoft partner out there. Depending on the country the rate can be from 1,5X to 3X the average partner rate.

Why do customers buy from MCS? There are a couple of reasons. One, for insurance. MCS can never walk away from a project run on Microsoft technology. Two, because Microsoft sales is pushing MCS hard in the customer and is even financing parts via Business Investment Funds. And three, because the technology is very experimental, and it is too risky to work with a partner.

Conclusions

Microsoft services is probably 30% of the headcount of Microsoft and less than 2% of the profit of the company. Services for Microsoft is an investment. The P&L structure of a consulting services company is not as interesting as a P&L of a software or a cloud services company. Microsoft will never make consulting services the biggest part of the organization.

However, with IT buying happening more and more through business decision makers and customers going through digital transformation, Microsoft will need to be more on the forefront of creating new capabilities and solutions at their customers and will have a more vertical and business focused skills. Therefore, expect the services arm to grow in line with this strategy.

Lessons for Partners

Partners sometimes have difficulties in working with MCS. As a partner, If you are a systems integrator and you work on strategic and enterprise accounts, you will come across MCS. There will be co-opetition. Our view is that it is best to be transparent and upfront with MCS and to establish a good governance and active relationships.

For very large SI´s MCS will sometimes be more of a competitor. If you are a smaller SI but you work in the same account space our suggestion is to get close to MCS.

There are different working models with customers. MCS can prime and can contract a piece via fixed price from a partner. They can subcontract resources in T&M fashion. A partner can prime and have a Q&A piece from MCS.

Another angle is to proactively subcontract resources to MCS. The people a partner subcontracts to MCS will in general be working on modern technologies and that way learn on the job.

Opportunities arise as well in subsequent phases of MCS contracts as it is very difficult for MCS to be able to do the maintenance on projects they have delivered due to the very high rates they use.

Chapter 9. Define your strategy

In this chapter we will try to provide you with some guidance to be able to answer the following questions: [52]

- What am I going to be?
- Where am I going to play?
- What will be my value add and differentiation?
- How do I get there?
- At what cost?

Every partner company in the Microsoft ecosystem is looking at secular market trends, is looking at the speed at which those trends are happening in their customers' business and in their own business.

The speed of transformation in turn depends on the industry, geography and competitors. It is our finding that, basically, there are now four partner types: ISVs, Modern partners, Distributors and Asset heavy partners.

ISVs

The question - what am I going to be? - is probably the easiest to answer if you are an ISV. In 99 percent of cases you will remain an ISV and you won't be programmatically adding the other business models like project implementation, managed services or software resell. The

---

[52] The statements in this chapter have their underpinning based on the research in Refresh the Road Ahead which I published in July 2018. https://www.amazon.com/Refresh-Road-Ahead-Successful-Partnering-ebook/dp/B07FLNHKCJ/ref=sr_1_1?ie=UTF8&qid=1534182297&sr=8-1&keywords=refresh+the+road+ahead

only exceptions would be helping out in initial project implementations to get a partner started for example, providing a managed service for a very specific customized solution or enabling a customer via your CSP contract. However, this would always be to support your core ISV business.

We have seen that ISVs are thinking about the following things:

Cloud architecture and lock in. Either ISVs still need to move their solutions to the cloud or they have already moved their solutions to Azure. What they worry about is the dependence on and lock in on the Microsoft platform.

Cloud and new capabilities. ISVs that have moved to the cloud are considering how to use features that the Microsoft cloud platform provides like AI and Big Data in their future product strategy.

Public Cloud Pricing. Depending on the type of solution and type of industry some ISVs make heavier use of Azure than others. An SMB ERP in the cloud uses a lot less Azure than a media streaming solution for the media industry. In this second case, a couple of cents difference between Azure and AWS can have a big impact.

Geo focus. All ISVs we have interviewed have a regional or global aspiration. What is different is the level of maturity and execution. If there is one area where Microsoft could help ISVs it is to help them effectively go abroad.[53]

---

[53] Microsoft does not seem to have a framework, a methodology, the resource focus and all the right incentives in place to effectively do this. The most successful cases we have seen is because Microsoft corp made introductions to the field or

Indirect sales channel. All ISVs are working or planning to work via partners. The maturity levels are different. From accidental connections and projects to fully blown high cost strategies via existing distributors like for example Techdata or Ingram.

Pricing models. ISVs are using different pricing models. Even ISVs that have not moved to a cloud delivery model have in some cases moved to a per user pricing. Some have monthly models, other have yearly models. Some bill on a per month basis, others bill one or three years in advance.

To answer the questions that we started our chapter with for ISVs

- What am I going to be? In general, most ISVs know what they are and what they want to be, what value they provide for which type of customer in which segment and industry. They might add adjacent functionalities or industries.
- Where am I going to play? This question for ISVs is more related to geography.

---

pushed a specific ISV. This is ad-hoc and is not a scalable model. The ideal model would be that Microsoft sits down with an ISV to understand what solution they have or want to build and deeply understands the technical aspects, the solution value add, the industry and segment etc. Then Microsoft should help in understanding how much potential market is out there, help with the business plan, prioritize geographies, help in selecting implementation and resell partners, get the ISV connected with the local field org and incentivize the local field sales org. In order to do this Microsoft would need a team of high level consultants on both the business and technical side who cannot be measured on the in fiscal year revenue they generate. Helping an ISV go abroad and be successful cannot be measured in a 12 months period.

- What will be my value add and differentiation? Most ISVs have a clear understanding of what they offer, to which customer segment, industry and who their competition is.
- How do I get there? This question for ISVs is more related to how quickly they have moved to cloud based pricing and cloud technology.
- At what cost? It is difficult to give any real cost estimates as it depends on the complexity of the solution you are building. The numbers can range between one and a couple of million dollars for building a horizontal quick intranet solution, to rewriting an ERP SMB solution for the cloud to building a cloud brokerage solution.

The Modern Partner

While ISVs might have the cleanest model and clearest strategy we have found that services companies and companies that come from a majority resell background are all moving into the same direction.

They are all considering a mix of services (business consulting, systems integration, managed services), they are looking at IP and they are starting to include reselling Microsoft cloud services.

That is why we have pulled them all together into one category which we call the modern partner. In this category we have put software resellers like LSP´s, managed services providers, systems integrators, business consultants, dynamics partners, solution partners and global SI´s.

We will use the business characteristics model to review some of the possible strategy options. [54]

Cloud revenue. As discussed before all modern partners are aware that they need to move to cloud projects as much as possible. On prem will survive in very large customers with a lot of legacy and maybe in some regulated industries.

The SMB segment will move to the cloud in its entirety. LSP´s are hiring cloud architects, presales consultants, are investing in offshore services capabilities and are buying services companies.

Managed services providers are including more public and hybrid cloud either as a delivery mechanism for their end customer services or as part of their service portfolio.

Devops and automation are becoming key areas for investment. Systems integrators are all over the place. Some are more advanced than others.

Business consultants tend to be at the same level as general SI´s with their level of cloud skills. Dynamics partners have been behind specifically in Azure skills but have been playing catchup over the last couple of years.

We would suggest setting a goal for the % of cloud revenue you want to generate short medium and long term. You will want to be aggressive in order not to fall behind your competition.

Business model. What we have seen is the modern partners are looking at all four pillars of the modern partner business model. Projects, managed services, IP and resell. Depending on your starting point and where

---

[54] This model is discussed in detail in Refresh the Road Ahead.

you want to go there are different levels of focus on the different business models.

Historically smaller SI's, solution partners, business consultants and Dynamics partners were heavier on the project side and maybe had some managed services but not as a core business. The Dynamics partners were used to reselling software with high margins, as this part of the Microsoft business had a different history. They have had to adjust to lower software resell margins, but most have expanded into CSP resell of other Microsoft solutions like O365 and Azure.

SI's in general did not resell any Microsoft software as the margins were not interesting plus Microsoft did only allow certain partners to resell. In some smaller countries some of the existing solution partners were also software resellers.

If you are a project services-based company (what Microsoft calls solution partners, SI's or business consultants) you can move into managed services, IP creation and software resell. IP creation is on the one hand easy as you will have probably done projects from which you can re-use IP, either horizontal or vertical.

However, on a continuum, from reactive use to full blown solutions there are a lot of different scenarios and costs involved. The more you move to the right the higher the cost, the longer the payback time but if you are successful the higher the margin will be.

As a project services-based company the move into managed services can happen in different ways. The easiest way is on the back of projects you have done for your customers where you also offer maintenance of software and potentially cloud services. However, keep in mind that when moving into managed services you need another type of skills, you need supporting infrastructure, you are moving to providing SLA´s, probably 7x24 support, etc. And you will need a minimum volume of business to pay for all this hard and soft infrastructure.

As a project services company you can move into resell via the CSP program. You can become an indirect reseller or a direct provider. If you work on large customers, most of these will already be a Microsoft EA customer and you will have few CSP resell opportunities as the customer will already own most of the licenses/cloud services plus you will not be able to compete on price.

If you work in SMB and potential greenfield customers proactively reselling via CSP is probably worth your while. Keep in mind as well that to most project-based companies reselling cloud services doesn't come natural to their sales force.

If your model is largely resale you will want to move into services, projects and managed services. However, if you are largely a reseller you will have a workforce focused on short term sales transactions and on operational excellence. You will need to hire the technical resources to move into projects. You will need to create project management capabilities, you will need to create project accounting capabilities in your financial systems. You will probably need to hire new sales people. You will need to attract the necessary technical talent. A quicker way to do this is to buy existing services companies which is what some LSP´s are doing.

We suggest that you model different scenarios for the four business models. There are different margins depending on the type of business. Investment and

payback time are different. The risk profile of the different business is different. After modelling decide on how much, if any, of the four business models you would like to be doing and set targets for the short, medium and long term.

Geographic focus. For the modern partner, how the geographic strategy decision might be influenced in this new world has to do with how quickly the market will move to solutions bought via market places and how quickly customers will move to buying full blown SaaS solutions. In order to have solutions in market places you need IP. Then there are the strategies that have always been in place like follow a customer that needs support abroad.

There are different strategies for going abroad. The more direct control you want the more expensive. P2P with likeminded partners is a potential low-cost option. If you have IP you can start to think about creating an indirect channel.

Specialization. There are different ways to specialize. Technology based, innovation focused, functional, industry, etc. With the rapid advances of technology, it will be more difficult to be and remain a generalist except for the really big players. As the world moves more to ecosystems and as we will see more fluid P2P constructions it will become easier to connect to other specialized partners to provide an end to end solution.

Intellectual property. Microsoft is pushing the IP lever hard however without providing much help with the what and the how and not a lot of support financially.

We see IP along a continuum. From IP is a reactive strategy to a more proactive strategy, to re-use of technical artifacts, to re-use of business artifacts, to solutions that are in the OCP catalogue, to uploading your solutions to a Microsoft market place, to being a full-blown ISV.

Building IP is expensive. Before you get in too deep, use modern management philosophies like design thinking and lean startup for the IP you are creating. Think about the existing people profiles you have versus the profiles you need.

Customization. In the cloud world, in general, you want to stay away from customization. We are moving from customization to personalization. Personalization is adjusting standard settings or capabilities in the product for a customer.

The challenge here Is that a lot of customization for a customer means more consulting revenue and more maintenance revenue for the partner. Everything which is a commodity customers will want to customize as little as possible. There is no competitive advantage to be had with O365 or with an ERP solution if your competitors can buy that same solution. For their core business, where the customers have a competitive advantage, the customer will build and customize solutions.

Customers will want customization only in areas where they want to have a competitive advantage. In all other areas they will drive for standardization with minimum personalization.

Customer segment. What we did not realize enough before writing this guide was the impact the customer segment has on other strategic decisions. If you focus on SMB you need to scale. In order to scale you need to standardize. You need to make it repeatable. You need to automate. You need to move to per user monthly pricing.

You will also find yourself working more with the Microsoft OCP organization and the tele sales teams. When you work with large customers you will deliver more customized solutions. You will still be able to get paid for a project with part upfront payments. You will engage with the enterprise unit, ATU, STU, CSU and with Microsoft services.

Your strategic choice of customer segment drives impact on standardization, pricing, scale, pricing models and who to engage with at Microsoft.

We will try to give some direction for answering the key questions for modern partners.

- What am I going to be? Think carefully about what you are going to be, in which business models you are going to play, what the cost of these business models are, what it will take you to get there and what the risk profiles are of these business models.
- Where am I going to play? Think about the customer segments, the vertical industries and geographic scope.
- What will be my value add and differentiation? The times of being everything to everybody are gone. Think about how you add value, where do you specialize? How do you differentiate from your competition and make sure that Microsoft understands why and how you are different?
- How do I get there? Model carefully and look at all your options. Do not blindly follow what Microsoft tells you to do. Microsoft field

employees have limited understanding of partner P&L´s.
- At what cost? This depends on the amount of transformation you need to do and on your sources of financing. Do you need to finance out of operations? Can you attract outside capital? Will you go for debt financing?

The Distributor

Distributors are transforming rapidly in becoming cloud brokers, are hiring consultants to help other channel partners with their cloud presales and are providing digital marketing services for partners that don't have those capabilities.

The Asset Heavy provider

We have separated out what we call the asset heavy providers like hosters, housing companies and Telco's. Being asset heavy not necessarily in the long term is an advantage specifically with a world moving to a few hyperscale providers and a world were infrastructure will be run by software.

We have summarized the partner strategy options in table 4.

Partner Type	Subtype	Partner strategy topics
ISV		Cloud architecture and lock in? Public Cloud Pricing Geo focus. How to build my indirect sales channel? How to use new cloud enabled functionalities like AI? Experiment with pricing models
Modern Partner = Services, IP and Resell partner	Software reseller, MSP, Systems Integrator, Business Consultant, Dynamics partner, Solution Partner, Global SI	How to get to high levels of cloud related revenue? What business models are attractive to me? Projects, managed services, IP creation, resell? Where do I play geographically? Do I build P2P partnerships or even an indirect channel for my IP? Do I specialize? On what and where? Do I build IP? What do I build? Why? Where to start? What will it cost? How do I sell and distribute my IP? Do I try to stay away from customization or is it key to what I do and what my customer segment wants? What is my customer segment? SMB or Enterprise? What size SMB? What vertical Market?
Distributors		How do I move from very low margin HW and SW resale to cloud? What cloud brokerage capabilities do I buy versus build? What other value add services can I provide to my partners? Do I start to play a role with direct end customers in support of my channel?
Asset heavy providers	Hosters, Telco's	Where do I play versus Hyperscale clouds? Do I compete or partner or both? What is the long-term strategy for my assets?

Table 4. Partner Strategy options II

Conclusions

We cannot give a one size fits all answer for some of the questions that we asked in the beginning of the chapter. What we can do and hopefully have done is paint a picture of where the world is going, what the strategy options are for partners and what some of the key issues and questions are. One of the biggest challenges you will have as a partner is to decide which things you will have to stop doing.

Lessons for partners

Do not depend too much on Microsoft. Microsoft will change incentives, cancel products, change roadmaps, move people around, restructure from one year to the next, cancel programs and funding, etc. Rely on yourself and your own strategy while understanding where Microsoft is going long, medium and short term. Take advantage of what Microsoft offers you but let that never be such a large part of your business to put yourself at risk.

In the next chapter we will try to operationalize how to engage with Microsoft through the lens of two partner types. The modern partner and the ISV.

Chapter 10. Operationalize

In this chapter we will give you guidance on how to operationalize your engagement with Microsoft.

Operationalizing your strategy with Microsoft

How to operationalize your strategy with Microsoft depends on the following overarching drivers.

- The customer segment you focus on.
- Single country or multi country focus.
- Your value add to Microsoft.

Customer segment

In the enterprise operating unit, you have strategic and enterprise accounts, in the SMC organization you have corporate and SMB accounts. The Microsoft account list is called the 'MAL', the managed account list. This list describes what segment the customers falls in.

Microsoft will not share the MAL in writing with partners, but it is our experience that a subset of the list is shared when you ask for it. Keep in mind that MCS does not necessarily follow the MAL 100 percent. They might decide that other customers are more strategic for them.

The engagement model with Microsoft is very different if you work on customers in the enterprise segment versus customers in the SMC segment.

Single country or multi country focus.

From an organizational design perspective working with Microsoft across different countries is easy. Once you have figured out your ideal engagement model of working with Microsoft in country A you can repeat the design for country B. The basic design of roles is the same for every country.

If you want to engage with Microsoft in another sub it is as easy as asking somebody you know in Microsoft to look up who is in a specific role in that country you want to engage with and then reach out. You do need to have a clear plan for why you are reaching out and what value you will be adding.

Your value add to Microsoft

You need to understand what your value add is to Microsoft. Your value add can lie in having more powerful relations in certain customers. In being an industry specialist, in having deep niche knowledge and ideally knowledge where Microsoft still needs to win market share.

Also think about the type of value add play you have. Do you focus only on an efficiency play or do you have a creation play? An efficiency play would be focusing on O365, M365, Azure IaaS, Datacenter, etc. A creation play would be generation of new solutions for customer using Azure PaaS, Big Data, AI, IOT etc.

Partners with an efficiency play focus more on the IT side of the end customers and partners with a creation play tend to be working with IT but also with line of business, innovation and other functional areas.

When you have an efficiency play you are most interesting to Microsoft when you can add new customers or move on prem customers to the cloud. Microsoft is focusing more and more on creation plays and partners that play in that space.

If you as a partner work in more 'old style' workloads or in workloads where Microsoft clearly feel they have won the battle, you will not get any love from Microsoft. They are happy to have you as a partner, you can use all the facilities they give you via the partner network, get incentives, go to events, but you will not get any proactive management and support.

You need to be very clear in what your value add is to Microsoft. Choose a limited number of areas.

Should you engage with Microsoft?
Engaging with Microsoft has a cost. There is the basic cost of becoming a member of the partner network, getting to competency levels etc. You need to think about what level of alignment you need and what you can afford. If you are not providing any of the value adds mentioned above to Microsoft maybe you want to think twice before investing a lot of time and money in proactively engaging with Microsoft.

Engaging in the enterprise segment.
In the enterprise segment you have to engage with a myriad of teams and roles. The account team unit, the specialist team unit, the customer success unit and the Microsoft services division, MCS.

In the enterprise segment on the accounts you have in common with Microsoft you need to understand who the account manager is and who the ATS's (account technical specialists) are that cover those accounts.

Then you need to understand who in the specialist sales organization (STU) covers the customer. This can be multiple people from multiple solution areas (modern workplace, apps & infra, data & AI and business apps).

You also need to know if your customers are covered by the CSU, who are focused entirely on consumption of Microsoft cloud services in those customers.[55]

Then it is wise to engage with Microsoft services as well. MCS is organized by verticals both in sales and delivery. Those verticals are managed by vertical sales managers and your account can have a services sales account manager assigned.

Then, there are also services solution sales professionals, Sssp's, that are solution area aligned and could be touching your account. On the delivery side there are industry aligned service delivery managers who have account delivery executives reporting to them. Technical account managers are also aligned by customer.

On a relatively large customer you can have ten or more people at Microsoft to engage with. On global accounts it can be even more.

It is our suggestion that you map out all the Microsoft people that are involved in your accounts. The enterprise account manager is the one role with the overall

---

[55] We have seen the CSU mostly focused on Azure with only some countries having resources focused on modern workplace in FY18.

Microsoft vision of the account, but you might get more traction via some of these other roles. In our experience, it will be more you connecting with Microsoft than the other way around. Keep them informed of what you are doing in those accounts. Share your account plans with Microsoft. It is our experience that this proactive transparency pays back.

The OCP enterprise channel manager is not an opportunity manager for a partner generated opportunity. Nor does the enterprise channel manager review your pipeline of Microsoft opportunities.

The enterprise channel manager, at least in theory in FY18, was assigned to a vertical industry. For that industry s/he needs to build a plan based on market opportunity. If there are co-sell ready solutions from partners for that industry vertical, then the Channel manager should generate a go to market plan for the industry/solution combination.

If there are no solutions for the market opportunity, then the channel manager should go back to the Build With organization to make sure that Build With has the creation of solutions for this vertical opportunity on its radar. The channel manager also distributes new opportunities according to the documented partner specialization.

In the enterprise segment it is our suggestion to keep the relevant channel managers in the loop as well but don't expect the channel manager to manage all the multiple internal connections in other departments on your behalf.

Engaging in the SMC segment

SMC for Microsoft is corporate accounts and SMB accounts. Both the corporate and SMB segments are managed by a Microsoft sales manager. The corporate segment might have some local account executives although the tendency is more toward tele sales engagement.

Both the corporate segment and the SMB segment have support from the remote tele sales engines which have both account management and specialist roles.

The OCP sell with organization has territory channel managers for the corporate and SMB segments. There are more channel managers assigned to the corporate and SMB segment than to the enterprise segment.

The SMC segment is more partner oriented than the enterprise segment. The direct sales resources are more limited and are in a remote capacity and MCS is not really interested in this segment except maybe for selling some premier support contracts.

Make plans with the sales manager for corporate and SMC, be in contact with the Microsoft tele sales people, even better go and visit them, and engage with your tele sell with team.

Like the enterprise channel managers, the territory channel managers are not opportunity managers for a partner generated opportunity. Nor does the territory channel manager review your pipeline of Microsoft opportunities.

However, the territory channel managers do share opportunities that are generated either via inbound marketing, marketing campaigns or via the tele sales centers.

Plan, Execute & Govern

Plan

If you plan to go beyond a basic engagement model, then take some time to put your strategy with Microsoft on 'paper'. We hope we have given you enough input on the Microsoft strategy, plans and execution for you to understand if you should make a specific plan with Microsoft.

There is no standard format that Microsoft imposes on its partners. Make it crisp. Explain what your company does, which (solution) areas you are focusing on, which verticals, which segments and which customers.

Explain what type of company you are, and what your strategy is across the spectrum of projects, managed services, IP and resell. You can explain your geo focus, how much your cloud related revenue is and what your targets are around cloud, which Microsoft customer segment you focus on, if you are focused on customized solutions or standardized solutions, what pricing mechanisms you use, what type of specialization you have of where you will be focusing your specialization and what IP you have and what IP plans you have.

Make sure to write your plan in 'Microsoft language'. Use their terms and definitions. Also explain what you need and which 'asks' you have for Microsoft. A couple of slides suffice. Don't make it too long or too complex. Always share those slides after meetings. Have paper copies of those slides with you to share during and after a meeting.

There is no single 'owner' for your plan in Microsoft. The most interested person should be your PDM if you have one but discussing the plan with just the PDM does not suffice. You will want to socialize your plan with more people.

The build-with lead, the GTM people if applicable to your strategy, the sell- with lead and either enterprise channel managers or territory channel managers. If you work in the enterprise space you will want to socialize your plan with the ATU leads, the STU managers and maybe some of the CSU managers as well. The higher you can get the better.

If you can get your plan 'sponsored' by senior leadership, it will have more impact. That sponsor could be the OCP lead and, in some cases, even the country GM. This is, of course, only possible for certain partners.

Then, don't forget the Business group leads. They own the overall performance of the solution areas for the subsidiary all up. From enterprise to SMB. They have the helicopter view. They also have visibility of funding and, in some cases, are the requestors for larger funding from the area or corp and approvers locally.

The more people that know you and your company the better. But you have to be crisp and you must add value. It is probably worthwhile to create a governance matrix where you detail who in your organization is supposed to meet whom at Microsoft and how many times a year.

Your planning horizon cannot be longer than one fiscal year with the Microsoft field. Only if you engage with pure corp organizations in some cases a multi-year business plan can be established and sponsored.

Your plan has two objectives. One is to explain and manage the ongoing business you have with Microsoft. The other objective is to come away with one, two or maybe three key 'actions' that can bring additional benefits to you and Microsoft as a win-win. We will call these the 'big rocks'.

Your plan should have goals both on the ongoing business and on the big rocks. Ideally Microsoft buys in on those goals.

Execute

Microsoft will not be owning your plan. The best you can expect is some individuals at Microsoft co-owning some of the actions in your plan.[56] You will need to own the daily, weekly and monthly actions. Be proactive. Make sure your whole organization is proactive. Inform Microsoft of advances.

Govern

Governance is what will make you successful. Define your governance matrix. This is like a multi-level sales matrix. You need to define who needs a relationship with whom. How that relationship is established. How often these people need to meet. What the objective and expected outputs of those meetings should be. Agree this matrix with Microsoft.

---

[56] The only exceptions are some of the very large partnerships that have alliance managers assigned on both sides.

This is important as you are asking people for their time. Get those meetings in the calendar, at least for two quarters. The more senior level meetings you will want to get into the agenda for the whole fiscal year. Review your governance model execution, at least, once a month.

Conclusions

Making partnerships successful is hard work that requires ongoing effort. Partnership KPI's are not part of the ongoing business KPI's. The people that do the hard work in the background are not normally the people that get the 'photo op' moments when outcomes are successful.

If you want to be successful in a partnership, you cannot abdicate the strategy and the management of that partnership to the alliance person. It needs to be a top down and bottom up approach.

Executing on a partnership strategy is the responsibility of the CEO, the CMO, the Practice managers, the CTO and partner roles. Everybody in your organization that has something to do with Microsoft needs to be making the partnership successful on a day by day basis.

Lessons for partners

How to operationalize your strategy with Microsoft depends on the following overarching drivers: the customer segment you focus on, single country or multi country focus and your value add to Microsoft.

You need to reflect on how much you should invest in operationalizing your strategy and execution with Microsoft. It is better to have a simple plan and execute than to have a complex plan that ends up in a drawer. The best way to guarantee that you execute on your partnership plan is to define a governance model and to review the performance of that model, at least, once a month.

Chapter 11. Best Practices & Challenges in working with Microsoft

In this chapter we will try to give some guidance of what to do and what not to do when working with Microsoft.

General best practices

Read, read, read.
To understand where Microsoft is going, do your homework. Study and read what Nadella says as this will give you a view a couple of years out.

Network, network, network
You can do all the right things, understand the Microsoft strategy, know the organization structure and setup, have a great company with great people, have the right products and capabilities, etc. In the end these are hygiene factors. You need to network.

Go to a lot of events. Establish your governance matrix and actively plan your networking. Make sure that all key people in your company do the networking and not only the person responsible for the Microsoft relationship. Sponsor Microsoft events.[57] Become a member of the

---

[57] Microsoft is a company with a lot of marketing dollars however these dollars are extremely centrally managed within very tight program guidelines. The local Microsoft leadership will be very

local IAMCP chapter. The IAMCP is the International Association of Microsoft Channel Partners.[58]

Understand the agenda of the individual(s) you are meeting with.

Microsoft from the outside seems like an easy company to manage. Not at all. Microsoft is a very complex company with an extremely broad set of products and offerings.

Microsoft competes with the whole world, from enterprise to entertainment. Because of this complexity, it is key to design a working model as a partner that focusses on the right things, the right people and the right outcomes.

There are many people at Microsoft and they are all responsible for their limited piece of the pie. Every person at Microsoft has an agenda that needs to be pushed. Depending who you meet with they will push their own agenda. As a partner you need to understand that agenda.

---

grateful for any sponsor money coming in to their local events and this gives you access to senior local leadership.

[58] The chapters have different maturity levels depending on the country. In some countries the IAMCP might not even exist. Here you will find a lot of different partners that have been working with Microsoft for a long time and who can give you all the insights and tips and tricks. Remember, it is an association, not a service bureau. You get out of it what you put into it. Membership costs are very low, in most countries comparable to the cost of two business lunches. It is run by volunteers, people like you and me, so remember that when you expect a certain level of service.

Simply ask the question. What is important for you? How are you measured? How can I help you reach your goals?

Be in the driver's seat

Microsoft employees are very busy. The business is complex. They have a lot of internal meetings. There are a lot of internal control systems and scorecards. One sometimes wonders how they can still have time to see customers and partners.

This means that as a partner you need to be in the driver's seat. Don't expect Microsoft to drive you. Some people might contact you regularly, but these are maybe not the right people. You need to understand who all the players are and drive the right governance.

Explain yourself in Microsoft's language

Everything you present to Microsoft, make sure that you present in a language they understand. Use their acronyms. That will make the conversation a lot more fluent. Microsoft has many partners they can work with. Be the one that is easy to work with.

Help Microsoft people be successful

Sometimes small things can make a difference. Understand the scorecard of the individuals you work with. Understand where they need help.

Sending a mail to the persons manager or managers manager from time to time when s/he has helped you out is a very small effort and will be appreciated.

Be transparent and honest
Be open and transparent at what you are good at and what you are not good at. Don't sell smoke and mirrors. You might have initial traction, but it will backfire dramatically.

Gives, gets and asks
I see some partners that, when they are finally in front of more senior Microsoft people, they start presenting and explaining all the wonderful things they do and then leave the meeting empty handed.

You need to explain what you do but use a large part of the meeting to talk about things that are not working in the relationship, what you are giving Microsoft and what you are getting back versus what you expect back and have at least one 'ask' at the end of your meeting. Most senior Microsoft execs like to get their hands dirty and will do a genuine effort to help you.

Think Partner2Partner
It is impossible to cover all the Microsoft platforms and all the Microsoft products. If you want to bring end to end solutions to your customers, you have to work with other partners. Be open, be honest, be transparent, think win-win. There are a lot of partners out there who have that mindset and you might be missing out on a bigger piece of the pie.

Don't rely on Microsoft, rely on yourself
Microsoft is a great platform which can benefit you and your company if you make the right use of that platform. Set the right expectations. Don't depend too much on Microsoft for leads, incentives, programs, support. Things might and will change. Sometimes for the good and sometimes for the bad.

Conclusions
For all but the biggest companies in the world the power balance in the relationship with Microsoft will be on Microsoft´s side, independent of how much Microsoft will tell you how much they value partners.

Microsoft provides great technology, great resources and is one of the more partner-oriented companies out there compared with their peers. Partnering with Microsoft can be great, but you need to think about how much you want to invest into the relationship.

Lessons for partners
Partnering with Microsoft can bring a lot of benefits. But you must be smart about it. First, question yourself about what you want to get out of the partnership with Microsoft.

Then ask yourself how interesting you are for Microsoft. If you think that there is a win-win, then think about the best steps to engage with Microsoft considering your own strategy and business characteristics.

'Design´ your engagement strategy, execute and follow up.

I hope I have been able to help you get started on your journey with Microsoft or if you are already a partner I hope that this guide helps you get to even better results with Microsoft.

Acronyms

AI: Artificial intelligence

AI+R: AI + Research, engineering group led by Harry Shum.

ASG: Applications and Services Group

ATU: Account team Unit

AWS: Amazon Web Services

AM: Account manager

BIF: Business investment funds

CAM: Corporate accounts managed

CAM-E: Corporate accounts managed by EPG

CAM-S: Corporate accounts managed by SMS&P

CFO: Chief Financial Officer

CIF: Cloud Investment Funds

COE: Correction of Error or Center of Excellence

CPE: Customer and partner experience (CPE).

EMEA: Europe, Middle East and Africa

EPG: The enterprise and Partner group

FTE: Full Time Equivalent

ISV: Independent Software Vendor

KPI: key performance indicator

LSP: Licensing Solution Partner

M&O: marketing and operations

MBD: Microsoft Business Division

MDG: Microsoft Devices Group

MGX: Microsoft Global Exchange now called Ready.

MYR: Mid-year review process

NDS: Nokia´s Devices and Services Business

OCP: One Commercial Partner Organization

OEM: Original Equipment Manufacturer

OSD: Online services division

PAC: Partner Advisory Council

PAM: Partner account manager

PCMM: partner channel marketing manager

PDM: Partner development manager

PMA: Partner marketing advisor

PRISM: Priority setting meetings

PSE: Partner sales executive.

PTS: Partner technical specialist

ROB: Rhythm of Business

SKU: Stock Keeping Unit

SMC: Small Medium and Corporate

SMSG: Sales, Marketing and Services group

SMS&P: Small and Mid-Market Solutions and Partners

SPLA: Service Provider License Agreement

SPOC: Single Point of Contact

STB: Server and Tools business group

TLI´s: Transformational Leading Indicators

WDG: Windows & Devices Group

WHI: Work Health Index

WPC: Worldwide partner conference or WPC now known as Inspire.

www.ingramcontent.com/pod-product-compliance
Lightning Source LLC
Chambersburg PA
CBHW020447220526
45464CB00002B/892